I0087514

F*CK A LABEL

A DIGITAL MARKETING MANUAL FOR MUSICIANS

KYREE J HOLLIS

DISCLAIMER

All of the content in this book is verified and organized to the best of our knowledge. This book is to guide upcoming musicians on how to push their music through social media platforms. The author has put a lot of effort into writing this book. Therefore, the author disclaims any form of liability, loss, or damage that may arise when using the content of this ebook. Hence, you are using this information at your own risk.

DESCRIPTION

This digital era changed the method of marketing for brands and other services. Music is not left out as the internet has changed the marketing strategies of new music. Upcoming and well-known musicians have decided to use social media platforms as a tool for connecting with their audience. However, the strategies deployed by these musicians may not favor them in the digital world. This book contains all the techniques required to conquer every challenge encountered by musicians in the process of marketing their music.

TABLE OF CONTENTS

Tik Tok

Music promotion on YouTube

DIGITAL MARKETING FOR MUSICIANS

Pushing good music to the right audience is one of the major challenges faced by upcoming music artists. Every musician works tirelessly to maintain a cordial relationship with their audience. Still, some of their efforts seem to yield poor results due to the type of marketing strategies deployed by them. Developers are coming up with impressive software applications, to help musicians connect with their right audience. Every artist that wishes to stay useful in the music industry should see this as an opportunity to increase their fan base. As a musician, you should show more concern on your fan base, because without having a strong fan base, your music may not go viral. Millions of music lovers are online searching passionately for suitable music that will match their mood. You can take advantage of this and push your music across several platforms and connect with the right audience.

Musicians with good music concepts can easily go viral on social media. Since about 4.5 billion people from the entire world population now use the internet, musicians can easily connect with their audience if they deploy a creative approach towards the digital world. Social media platforms are the best channel for musicians to connect with the right audience since about 3.8 billion people use social media to communicate with their loved ones. You can utilize this advantage and get your music trending across several platforms. To achieve this, you will have to connect with influencers or take up the task yourself.

Skills required by upcoming musicians to do digital marketing themselves

Every upcoming musician that wishes to push their song across the internet world must possess many digital skills. These digital skills will enable the artist to stand out. Since the internet world involves a lot of competition from talented musicians, you should develop digital skills to push you ahead of others. Some of these skills will take your musical career to the next level;

1. Storytelling abilities

Almost every social media handle ranks video posts based on the description attached to it. Your ability to tell a story matters a lot. You may decide to upload images or a write up on your Instagram story. For instance, your storytelling skills will enable you to build a better write up. Every good story must contain an impressive beginning, engaging body, and a satisfying conclusion.

2. Understanding social media ads tactics

This digital skill is essential for every upcoming artist necessary, and musicians with this skill are always ahead of others. To run any social media ad, you should have a good knowledge of ads; otherwise, your efforts will be fruitless.

How to run successful ads on every social media platform

Every social media platform has its ad method. However, as an upcoming musician, you should at least note the following about social media ads;

- **Know your targeted audience:** Learning more about your audience will stand as a guide towards a successful ad campaign. As a musician, you should consider channeling your ads towards a younger age demographic. Also, the location of your audience is necessary. If you decide to sing for a particular country or region, direct your ads to that region, and gain the attention you seek.

- **Control your financial budget:** Social media ads require finance to push your ads to the right destination. However, defining your ads will give you an insight on how to plan out your budget. Let your budget focus on impressing and engaging your audience. With this method, you can always control your ads.

- **Test your ad to boost performance:** After making your ads, you should not allow the social media platform to execute the whole job. Test your ads to monitor its performance.

- **Create a mobile-friendly ad:** Since most social media apps are designed to be mobile-friendly, create an ad that works better on mobile devices.

- **Use an organic post to boost your ads:** Your ads can still travel wide, but organic posts will give your ad potential to overpower other ads, and your videos or photo ads will reach your desired audience.

1. **Communication skills**

   You will require communication skills to keep your audience engaged. After making a post, you should be at the comment section to interact with your audience. You will need communication skills to keep the conversation engaging.

2. **Mobile marketing skills**

   This skill is of high demand in the digital world. Since most people access social media platforms, blogs, and other web pages with their mobile devices more than computers, you should learn all the strategies required in mobile marketing. You should gain background knowledge of traffic analytics, mobile development, mobile designs, and other skills that relate to mobile marketing.

3. **Creative thinking**

   As an upcoming musician, your approach towards social media platforms should be different. Creativity can do a lot in your career. Your video uploads deserve a lot of creative content to engage your audience. And your abilities to create such content highly depend on your creative skills.

4. **Project management skills**

   This skill is essential to manage social media campaigns. As an artist, you need to deploy this skill to obtain a successful campaign. This management skill will enable you to direct your team or colleagues working on the same project with you to achieve a better result

Risk factors involved in digital marketing for musicians

When it comes to digital marketing, you should note some challenges that may stand as a risk factor towards a successful campaign. Many artists are uploading content per day to engage their audience. However, some other people tend to steal their work for their private businesses and individual interest. Therefore, you should note the following risk factors before uploading content on any social media platform.

Plagiarism: All the content coming to the internet is supposed to be unique and new. When you copy other peoples' written content and paste it as your project, the internet will mark it as plagiarism. The rightful owner of the content may sue you and get all of the credit coming from your effort. Finding a creative writer to boost your post with a 100 percent free plagiarism article might be difficult. However, you should develop creative writing skills, and use plagiarism online checkers like Grammarly, to ensure that your article is in the right shape.

Copyright infringement: Every content creator should know much about copyright infringements before creating content. This has to do with images, videos, text, or any other content that belongs to a particular individual or company. When you use such content without obtaining permission from the original owner, the internet might label your content with copyright infringement. Whenever copyright laws protect any content, you should learn to avoid such content as the owners will still lay claims on your hard work.

Audience dissatisfaction: Your music content should be made in a way to please the audience. Imagine the money involved in producing, editing, and recording a song, yet the audience tends to neglect your effort and focus their interest on other musicians. You might become frustrated and may give up on your dreams. Therefore, create music that will capture the interest of your audience.

Trademark infringement: Every musician needs to brand their music to stand different. And most of them work hard enough to protect their brand from theft. Impersonating another artist is a huge crime, and you may get banned from having access to your social media accounts. Therefore, seek collaborations with other musicians, and if they decline your proposal, find another.

Online Fraudsters: Upcoming musicians can be desperate to push their music to the top. Many online fraudsters tend to take advantage of this and devise a means of defrauding them. When you look out for music influencers on any platform, make sure that you are on the right track as many people will tend to stand as a huge wall between you and your success. Do not pay anyone to get you "label meetings" or to "listen to your music." This is one of the most prominent scams sought out against up and coming musicians.

Best social media platforms for Musicians

When it comes to digital marketing for musicians, a lot of effort will be needed from the musician. Before the digital era, musicians preferred to engage their audience via radio stations. However, since the world embraced the digital age, musicians find it easier to reach out to their audience without stress. Marketing fresh music on social media requires a positive attitude from the musician to the audience. Musicians should consider the following social media platforms while trying to create an impact in the music industry.

INSTAGRAM

Instagram is one of the best platforms for musicians to showcase their music content in the world. As of 2018, Instagram has exceeded over a billion users, with 71 percent of its active users under the age of 35. This makes Instagram a better platform to connect with younger audiences. Most music lovers use this platform to connect with their desired artists. A good musician with rich music content can easily go viral via Instagram. Connecting with people via this platform may require some technical approach. Artists should build and maintain a cordial relationship with music promoters and Instagram influencers to assist in growing their fan base. When your music is good enough, some promoters may decide to post it on their feed, and this action will attract more followers and more views to the artist. What this implies is that music artists should focus on creating better music content, as the content of their music will determine their success in the music industry. To make your music travel beyond your expectation via Instagram, you will have to deploy the following strategies;

1. **Release quality audio**

   Your voice matters a lot. Before uploading a soundtrack on your Instagram handle, ensure that your soundtrack is unique and engaging. Poorly structured music content may scare away your audience. Instagram followers consider a lot of things before following a musician and one of their major considerations on such a musician's musical content.

2. **Consistency is the Key**

   The Instagram audience always expects engaging content from their favorite musicians' every day. Since the platform has more than 500 million active users on a monthly basis, you can increase your fan base with rich, engaging content. As a musician, you may not be able to upload new music every day, but you can engage your audience with stunting photos, live videos, and inspiring images. You don't have to be an influencer to grow your audience. A daily creative post can expedite your engagement growth, but no matter the situation, don't be a boring musician on Instagram. If you don't know how to develop a creative post on Instagram, you can study the post of trending musicians of your choice, and use that as a reference point.

3. Review your audiences' opinion

Never neglect your audience. Accept both the praises and the critics. The truth is that no matter your effort to produce good music, some people will still criticize your effort. You will have to make time to go through the comment section and outline their view. Some comments may tend to piss you off, but no matter the situation, don't overreact.

4. Use the appropriate hashtag

Hashtag marketing is one of the best methods to reach out to more audiences on Instagram. The hashtag is so powerful that it can allow people outside your existing followers to discover your post. Almost every viral post on Instagram contains some useful hashtags. You don't just wake up to use any hashtag that pleases you. There is a need to do proper research on every hashtag you will attach to your post. Millions of Instagram users are searching for several topics using hashtags. You can utilize this opportunity and develop your following. While selecting your hashtags, endeavor to choose the ones that are useful and popular as well, but make sure that their popularity is limited to some extent. Instagram users will love to use the most popular hashtag to upload their posts. Using similar hashtags may limit your chances of appearing on the top search. You can use an analytic tool to discover the popular hashtags that relate to your post. The best analytic tool to execute this task is known as Iconosquare. You can also use the search icon to discover more popular hashtags that relate to your post. Since you can edit the hashtag, you can change them from time to time to maintain your post's validity on the search rank. You can also search for hashtags that other musicians are using and include them in your post.

5. Time your post

Almost every country has a different time zone, which will affect your audience's online presence. But you can use an analytic tool such as iconosquare to monitor your followers' activities on Instagram. This tool will stand as a guide towards managing the time difference of your audience.

6. **Apply a call to action**

   Make out time to follow some Instagram influencers and popular musicians. Like and comment on most of their posts, and draw their attention towards following your handle.

7. **Invest in Instagram ads**

   Running Instagram an ad requires a strategic approach to gaining a positive result. You don't just invest in ads when you don't know much about it. Since ads require money, you will have to apply caution to target your ads to the right audience.

How to run successful Instagram Ads

Instagram ads that make a post go viral, must consist of the following;

- **Ads must be channeled to the right audience:**

  Instagram and Facebook have similarities when it comes to targeting the right audience through advertising. You will need to have a clear definition of the type of audience that loves your music. You can use the audience of musicians that sing the same genre as you, to determine your audience. Your Instagram analytics contains existing demographics data that can help you channel your ads to the right audience. Using the right hashtags can also contribute to the success of your ads.

- **Ads must contain a lot of strategic hashtags**:
Every hashtag must consist of letters or emoji accompanied by the #symbol. Hashtags can boost your post to the right audience. However, your hashtag selection has to depend on the content you are about to upload. Also, develop creative hashtags that represent what your audience will be searching for. Learn to ignore every irrelevant hashtag. Instagram will likely hide every post that comes with an irrelevant hashtag.

- **Add creativity to your ad description**:
Don't just upload your ad without defining your purpose. You can describe the content of your ad with a creative story and appropriate keywords. Your ad requires two effective approaches to gain much attention. The first approach is to push your ad to top search, and the most important approach is to impress your audience with such ads. If your ads are impressive, your content will go viral within a short time.

- **Use Instagram statistics to rate the performance of your ads**:

  Every social media platform has data statistics that analyze how the audience reacts to your post. You can differentiate people's reactions between your organic post and paid ad post.

- **Test your ad Campaign:**

  Testing your Instagram ads will give you an insight into your audience's response to your post. You can proceed to run your test ads after establishing your benchmark ad. The best testing ad to use is the standard A/B split testing method. This type of testing method will enable you to test several Instagram ads against another ad.

- **Use the most engaging music video for your ad:**

  Before you conclude in your ad campaign, you must consider choosing some engaging content before anything else. You don't just run an ad on your every post, run your ads only on the engaging content. Engaging content will attract more clicks and views. Your following will grow as well.

- **Target your ads to countries with most Instagram users:**

  Before selecting your ads' destination, you must consider the number of active Instagram users in those countries. According to Statista, the US has 120 million active Instagram users, which were ranked as the country with the highest number of active Instagram users in the world. After the US comes India in second place with 88 million active Instagram users. India was quickly followed by Brazil, with 82 million active Instagram Users. You can select these countries or similar countries with a high rate of Instagram users. However, if your ad is meant to tackle a particular issue in a specific country, you should proceed to run your ad without this consideration.

8. Upload consistently on your story

The Instagram audience hates to follow an uneventful musician on Instagram. You don't just upload content on your feed alone; try to keep your followers engaged by uploading impressive pictures or stickers on your Instagram story. There are several ways to improve your Instagram story view, and they include;

- **Use Instagram stickers:**

  The platform is designed in such a way that its users can utilize a lot of engaging stickers to interact with their followers. Instagram stickers come in a different form. The poll stickers will enable your audience to choose for you. Let's take, for instance, if you're considering two nice beats for your new song, you can upload the two beats and request for their opinion using the poll stickers. Instagram also has a question sticker; this type of sticker will enable you to interact more with your audience. Question stickers allow your audience to ask you a question in their own story, and why you give answers to such questions, Instagram will notify the person that his/her question has been answered. You can get more story views through this approach. Location stickers will allow your audience to know your current location. You can use all the stickers on the Instagram story to keep in touch with your audience.

- **Sing without an instrument in a short Video:**

  If it is possible, repeat this routine every day. Every music lover will love to watch you perform without any instrument or beat. It just comes naturally at times. Since Instagram allows only 15 seconds of video per story, endeavor to keep the song short. However, if the video is longer than 15 seconds, you can add it up to the next story, but try as much as you can to keep your video short and engaging.

- **Showcase your previous work:**

  Tell people about your previous project. Some of your new followers might not know much about you, but your last project will enable them to learn about your music. This approach will attract more reactions to your previous works, and your audience will motivate you to embark on the next project.

- **Post consistently:**

  Never skip a day without uploading content on your Instagram story. When you engage your viewers with everyday story posts, they will be more likely to engage with your story. The more they engage with your story, the higher your regular Instagram post will show up on their feed.

- **Direct your viewers:** You can instruct your viewers on how to manage your Instagram stories. Your instruction has to come in this format;

How to drive success through the Instagram Story

Tap for more: This prompt format will enable your viewers to see more of the content. One good feature of this format is that your story viewers can visit your handle. You can easily gain more reactions on your regular feed posts.

Hold to Read: When your content is lengthy, you can advise your viewers to hold their screen as they read. This prompt format will enable your viewers to enjoy your lengthy story without being timed out by Instagram.

Get Ready To: Most people use this prompt often to inform their audience about future events. You can use this prompt to enable your fans to learn more about your next song, or any other big event that will be coming up. This prompt can also give your audience insight into the next slide.

9. **Use Instagram live video to engage your audience:**

Live video on Instagram has become so popular that almost every top musician and influencers engage their audience with it. You can use it to engage your audience as well. To go live on

Instagram, you will have to follow these steps;

- You can start by tapping on the camera icon; however, if you don't like this approach, you can swipe your screen to the right side on your feed.

- The next step is to tap the live icon at the bottom of your screen, then select the round icon that will show up.

- Select the emoji joined together and proceed.

- Now it is time to invite people to join your live video. At this stage, you should bear in mind that you cannot invite a follower who is not viewing your live video already. You can invite people by selecting the add icon.

- When your follower accepts your invitation, you will see them on the split-screen; however, if they decline your request, you will be notified.

10. Understand your followers

You need to analyze your daily post and discover which post got more reactions, more comments, and more follow back. The truth is that your audience may not love your everyday posts, and most of them are selective on contents that attract their interest. There are several ways of understanding the interest of your audience, you can do this by relating closely with them in the comment section, Instagram story, or Instagram feed. When you understand their interest or the type of song that stimulates your fan base, you can reorganize your regular Instagram upload to match with their interest. While considering the content to upload, you must consider your audience first, before considering yourself. Don't just upload a music video because the soundtrack pleases your hearing. You should endeavor to make inquiries from your audience before proceeding to upload. You can post this inquiry on your Instagram story, and it must be engaging and attractive.

11. Consider Photos more than videos

When it comes to Instagram users, photos are always preferred more than videos. Most people don't have the time to watch all your lengthy videos, but they can easily watch your pictures and move on to the next content. You can upload photos that best describe your career part. A creative background will attract more audience to your handle. While taking your shots, you should try to add creativity to it.

12. Borrow Ideas from your Competitors

Some of your competitors might be ahead of you because they are giving their followers engaging content. You can follow your competitor and borrow ideas from them. In borrowing ideas, what you should be considering is how to recreate the idea to be unique and different. You have to make it appear unique so that your competitor may not recognize that he/she is the brain behind the idea. Your audience will react positively to the idea.

13. Organize a viral Instagram contest

Instagram users love viral contests and give away. This method will serve as the gateway to quicker fame on Instagram. You can organize viral contests that will suit every age, race, sex, and profession. Don't be selective while making your plans for a viral contest. Being selective will limit your audience, and some of the audience that meets up with your demand may neglect to participate in the contest. You can use the raffle press to organize a giveaway contest.

14. Build your name

Your name matters a lot. Most popular musicians worked hard to get their names trending on every platform. Moreover, if you don't work hard to secure your brand name, another person may decide to use the same name. Instagram made a rule that does not allow two people to share the same username. As a result of this, you should work hard to secure your brand name before anything.

15. Check out if synchronizing your Facebook and Twitter to Instagram is more comfortable

Facebook and Twitter is a huge platform to engage your audience. But, if you would prefer to carry all your audience along, Instagram is the best platform. Instagram allows its users to sync their Facebook and Twitter into its activities. Once you sync your Facebook and Twitter into your Instagram account, your every post from Instagram will reflect on both Facebook and Twitter. However, Instagram, Facebook, and Twitter all have a different approach to engage their various audiences. Let's take, for instance, Instagram posts require hashtags to gain more traffic, but Facebook posts require fewer hashtags to generate the required traffic. This action will favor your post in one platform and may not favor it in another platform. Consider this decision very well before executing it.

Setting up a Giphy account

Your Instagram Stickers have to be unique and different. Therefore, you should consider setting up a Giphy artist account to brand your stickers. Our organization helps musicians in creating a catchy Gighy artist account. Visit http://www.theorendaagency.com/ and connect with our expertise for your professional Giphy account. Following the steps below will enable you to link your Giphy account to your Instagram;

Customize your unique music logo using Giphy, which we can always do for you.

Locate the Giphy mobile app on your phone and click on the plane like icon.

Select the Instagram icon and proceed.

The next line of action is to select either an Instagram feed or Instagram story.

Gifs can also be found by pressing the sticker button on the upper right hand corner of the screen when creating a story on instagram. Once you have your personal Gif created by The Orenda Agency, all you have to do is type in your keyword(s) and your Gif will appear.

Instagram Chat Bot

Like other social media platforms, Instagram also has a chatbot that allows you to keep effective communication with your followers, even offline. Before now, Instagram had a lot of chatbots that guarantee auto like, auto comments, auto-following, and a lot more actions. However, some owners of these bots were not officially recognized by Instagram, and their bots were shut down. But this did not stop some genuine bots from helping musicians and other Instagram users interact better with their audience. Therefore, for you to use the Instagram chatbot effectively, you will have to deploy these strategies. This is a very effective way to promote a campaign for a new releasing song. This method assists in you building your email list as well as retargeting those people who have direct messaged you and triggered the chat bot.

- Conclude on how you want to use the bot on your Instagram account.

- Visit http://www.theorendaagency.com/ and navigate to the contact us page.

- Request for your chatbot services and get the best services.

- Test runs your chatbot.

- Connect better with your audience.

Instagram story viewer automation

When it comes to Instagram story views, the approach deployed by musicians to gain more traffic to their daily posts is encouraging. Some of these musicians use Instagram story automation tools to gain more attention from fans. However, this tool is against the Instagram terms and conditions mapped out to guide its users on the dos and don'ts. As an upcoming artist, you should consider this tool to help your Instagram account gain more attention from people. This method will help in growing your followers, increasing profile impressions, and overall engagement. You can contact http://www.theorendaagency.com/ for the best story viewer automation management.

How to Boost your engagement through the Instagram Engagement Groups

Instagram engagement groups can help to boost your chances of going viral sooner than expected. These engagement groups tend to increase your followers, likes, and comments. However, finding a real engagement group might be challenging at times. There are two broad main Instagram groups, and they include:

Instagram round-up groups on other social media platforms: This group allows you to connect with their audience, and you will help you grow your following.

The best social media platform to find this group in is telegram.

DM Groups: This group can be found on Instagram, and each member of the group tends to grow and support one another within the platform. You can use this method to grow your following.

How to gain more attention on Instagram via influencers

Music influencers on Instagram stand as a bridge between the musicians and their success. Most influencers have invested a lot in building their network. Influencers work so hard to maintain their followers with engaging content. The first approach is to build an audience, and the main task is to maintain the following. As an artist, you can buy the services of these influencers and connect with their audience. Finding a music influencer on Instagram could be time-consuming and stressful. A lot of fraudsters tend to pose as music influencers hoping to defraud some desperate musicians. Always remember to contact them by their emails given in their bio or DM. You can also source a talent management firm, BUT before you proceed to send a direct message or email, verify if the promoter is genuine and reliable. Instagram influencers charge their clients based on the number of followers they have. However, finding an Instagram influencer with a less engaging audience may be difficult at times. Therefore, you should consider influencers with a large audience. You can demand the influencer's email address and send your proposal to it. But before you select your influencer for your song promotion, you will have to consider some of these factors;

- **Contact the right influencers**:

  Music influencers on Instagram are always unique and different from other promoters. You will need to carry out proper research to ensure that you're making the right choice. Selecting the wrong influencer will only create room for low response. Do a proper background check on the influencer before introducing your business plan to them.

- **Professionally approach the influencer**:

  While introducing yourself to the influencer, you should come professionally. Speak correct English and put all your words in order. You can always build a better relationship with influencers when you're always professional.

- **Verify their terms and condition before anything else**:

  Always remember to ask for a contract when

contracting business. If their terms and condition tally with your policy, you can proceed to contact them. However, if the specified terms and conditions are against your policy, you should consider finding another influencer.

The success story of Tory Lanez

Tory Lanez was born in Brampton, Ontario, Canada, on 27th July 1992. His real name is Daystar Peterson. After a while, his family relocated from Montreal, Quebec Province to Florida. While in Florida as a teenager, he developed an interest in rap music. He was inspired by popular musicians such as R. Kelly, Brandy among others. He loves moving around the street and his friends called him Lanes, and that was where he derived his stage name. Tory spent three years on the street, and his passion for Hip pop grew as days went by. He always wanted to be a different musician who can sing, rap, and perform every act related to music. Since Tory Lanez has a different view on music, he labeled his style of music as a swavey style. He worked so hard to push his way to the top. On 19th August 2016, He released an album titled *I told you*. Two songs from his surfaced on the billboard hot 100. *Luv* was ranked higher than *Say it*. He became so popular on Instagram after engaging his audience with several live videos. But on 31st March 2020, Tory Lanez decided to hold a live video, which he called quarantine radio. While on live chat with his followers alone, he had about 140,000 viewers, But when Drake appeared on the live video with Tory, his viewers increased to 310,000 viewers. Lanez testified that he gained 2.2million followers after the quarantine radio live video show.

From this story, you will observe that, when you connect with your following on your live video, you can gain positive results at the end of the day.

TIK TOK

Tik Tok was initially launched in September 2016, but it became popular after merging with music.ly on 2nd August 2018. The developers ByteDance created the platform to allow video creators to reach out to more audiences. Tik Tok is gradually becoming the newest internet sensation. Based on the way people are navigating to the platform, one could predict that the app could turn out to become modern Instagram in the future. Tik Tok has over 800 million active users with 41 percent of the user between the age brackets of 16 to 26. Every musician that wishes to go viral must be on this platform. The platform allows its users to upload a 15-second video of them. This app is a bit similar to Snapchat and Instagram, except that videos on Tik Tok are usually for public consumption. Musicians and artists have decided to use this platform more than any other platform, as it allows them to promote their music to a wider range of audiences. Unlike snap chat where your videos will appear like the Instagram story, Tik Tok is a better option for musicians. You can create a challenge on Tik Tok and gain a lot of reaction from the audience. Artist can go viral on Tik Tok if they apply the following strategies;

1. Consider Tik Tok before other Social Media Platforms

Tik Tok is the newest platform for musicians to connect them with a wider audience. If you are a musician and don't have a Tik Tok account, you are making a huge mistake. Once you are done with your music video, upload immediately to your Tik Tok channel. If you are yet to create a channel, you should follow this approach;

- Visit your Google play store or apple store and download Tik Tok.

- Open the app on your phone and sign up.

- Fill in your details accurately (especially your email id and phone number).

- Navigate to your profile and change your profile.

- You can add your YouTube channel to your Tik Tok account if you want.

- Then start uploading your videos on the platform.

2. Create an attractive profile

Every successful musician on Tik Tok has an attractive profile to engage his/her audience. As a musician, people will expect you to come different and dress in the latest fashion. Creating a boring profile is a way to tell your audience that you are not up to date with the new trends.. Therefore, before contacting influencers or organizing a challenge for your new song, endeavor to create an attractive profile that defines who you are, what you can offer to the audience, and a clear image that tells every visitor about your music intentions. Try to keep your username short and simple, build your brand name before anything else. The genre of your music matters a lot, maintains all your music in the same genre, and even if your music changes, ensure that you have to build a brand on that genre. Once your fans love you, they can easily accept anything new from you. Let's take, for instance, you may produce your first Tik Tok video showing your interest in nature. And your next video, you will tend to act funny. Some fans may love it, but most people that follow you because of their love for nature may unfollow you. Therefore, you ought to maintain a particular niche for a long time before switching.

3. Work with music influencers

You can follow a lot of music influencers on Tik Tok and collaborate with them. Finding a popular music influencer is not difficult on Tik Tok, but it may come with a price. Some of these promoters may be engaged with several activities, and you may receive less attention when you come unprofessional. When you introduce yourself to them, try to appear professional and always go straight to the point. Some may still ignore your message despite your effort to appear so professional. But when you experience such an attitude from an influencer, develop another creative approach towards capturing their interest. Tik Tok influencers have helped several musicians gain their fame within a space of time. Before contacting any Tik Tok music influencer, navigate to their TikTok account and verify how their audience reacts to their everyday post. This survey will give you an insight into the type of reaction you will gain from your influencer's promotion. The price required for music promotion differs from influencers. Every influencer considers the size of their audience before concluding on their promotion prices. However, most influencer loves to collaborate with artists who have engaging content to offer. Therefore, you should focus more on creating good music to gain their attention faster. Apart from requesting a paid promotion, you can plead to have music collaboration with them. Some may agree to this, while others may turn down your request. But no matter what their reaction might be, endeavor to try out your luck. After your music promotion with any influencer, wait for the reaction from his/her audience. If you are getting less attention, you will have to apply a call to action technique by notifying the influencer to create a means of redirecting his/her audience to your page.

4. **Consider scripting your actions before recording:** Never grab a camera to record yourself and upload on TikTok. Draft out a script that will stand as a guide towards your video records. When you write down your video action before executing, you will appear more professional, and the video content will be attractive and engaging as well. As an artist struggling to build your fan base, you should not behave like a popular celebrity. You should start small and focus.

Preparing for daily video recording

A good writing script should contain the following;

- **Dialogue:**

  Your dialogue consists of every word that will be pronounced in the video. You can decide to keep it short and engaging since Tik Tok only accepts short videos alone. Remove every irrelevant word from your dialogue and try to keep it simple. Adding ambiguous words to your dialogue will make it difficult for people to relate very well with you. Carrying out proper research before writing your dialogue will help you to build more relevant content. Let's take for instance; If you want to make a video about your music dance. You ought to find relevant words related to dance and work with them.

- **Action:**

  Action is necessary for every video as it tends to dictate your body movement. Make your action engaging and attractive. If it is possible, demonstrate your dialogue with your hands. Don't forget that some of your audience may be deaf, and only understand body movement. You use this technique to carry everybody along. While writing your action, you should try to keep it real and simple. Don't make the video appear so scripted with a complex action display. If you are still confused on how to put your action into writing, then listen up. Let's assume that I'm making an educational video to teach people how to dance my latest song. I will start by writing my action in this simple format; "Moving my right foot across my left foot while both my hands are in the air. Then, moving my head forward, my hands return to balance with my shoulders". From the above example, you will observe that my action is simple and can be obtainable. Your action must tally with your dialogue. However, you can make a video without dialogue and use your body movement to carry your audience along.

- **Character:**

    Just like the movie, characters are the backbone for every good video. Before making the video, conclude on the characters that you want to appear in the video. If you require more than one person, script the video to fit in your characters. However, you should consult your characters to prepare before the video shoot. Never inform them late; otherwise, the result may be bad and discouraging. Make sure that your characters can display engaging and attractive actions. Your entire focus should always be on how the audience will react to your video.

5. **Focus more on video content**

Tik Tok is all about visuals and less interest in the audio. However, your audio still needs to come with a high-quality sound. Endeavor to record your video with an HD camera or with a high-quality phone. Your followers can only relate well with your post when your videos are displayed in high visual quality. You can also work with a studio to cover this aspect. Bear in mind that your followers will always be expecting video content from you, so you may not necessarily need to visit the studio for your daily video recording, You can just use your phone to create an engaging content that relates to your vision about music.

6. Consider editing your videos outside Tik Tok

Tik Tok has an inbuilt editor that allows creators to add filters and effects to their video. You can use this technique to edit some of your videos.

How to Edit Videos Using TikTok inbuilt editor

If you prefer to edit your videos on Tik Tok, you should follow these procedures;

- Immediately you launch the Tik Tok app on your android or apple phone, you will be welcomed with interesting videos from several tik to users. However, you can start your video record by tapping on the "+" icon.

- The "+" icon will enable you to navigate to the video recording and editing section. This interface contains all the tools required to upload a video on Tik Tok.

- You can start by tapping on the record button to tape yourself.

- When you are done with the video recording, you can edit your video with the available filters and video effects.

- You can add background music to your video as well as a sound effect from the Tik Tok editor. Sound effects and background music will always boost the potentials of your video. But if you prefer to sing on your video, you may upload your videos without background music or sound effects.

Benefits of Editing your videos outside TikTok

However, taking your video edit outside the platform will enable you to gain access to more effects and filters. With video editing software like Filmora, you will have access to more than 300 video effects and a lot of filters to create more professional videos. Editing your videos out Tik Tok will give you access to the following features;

- **More filters**:

  Almost everybody on Tik Tok is using the limited filters made available by the platform to edit their video. You should come different and unique. You ought to learn video editing from professionals or YouTube tutorials, then apply the knowledge on your video. There are several video editors out there, you can check out the best video editor that you can use and proceed. Filters make your video appear unique and more engaging. It tends to change the original color of your video to something different and it will make your videos appear more pleasant to your audience.

- **More effect:**

  Tik Tok users love to watch videos with attractive video effects. Using the Tik Tok video effect will limit your abilities to access more interesting video effects. As an artist that wants to gain more followers from Tik Tok, you should consider adding related video effects to describe the content of your video. Video content with several unique features can easily attract more followers.

- **More sound effects and background music:**

  Use several sound effects to make your video look more real and engaging. Let's take for instance; if you want to make a video with a dog, and require the dog to bark in the video, and you were not happy with how it came out, you can use a dog sound effect to create the bark sound. However, the Tik Tok sound effect may just grant access to a commonly used barking sound effect. Using this effect on your video will make it appear like every other video on Tik Tok. But when you edit your video with a professional video editor, you can always have access to a variety of royalty-free sound effects and add a more professional sound to your videos. As for the background music, you can gain access to more suitable and engaging music tracks to back up your video. The background music must relate to your video content.

- **More tools:**

    As a music artist that wants to come different on Tik Tok, you will be required to use more advanced video editing tools to add creativity to your video.

7. Post a video every day

Every popular Tik Tok user almost has the same thing in common, they post at least one video per day. To meet up with this schedule may be time demanding, stressful, and require focus. But if you are consistent with your post on the platform, you can easily gain popularity with time. You must not be uploading a music video every day, but you can add creativity to your video uploads on Tik Tok and invest your time in unique content. You might just wake up in the morning, and you may appear confused on what to share with your audience. If you are running out of ideas, you should visit peoples' profiles and tap from their ideas. Read people's reactions to such a post, to see if your idea will yield positive results. Your daily videos have to keep your audience engaged. When they are impressed by your work, you will probably receive better follow back from them.

8. Apply call for action

Just like Instagram, you should apply the same approach to TikTok. Don't act like a strict person, or appear to scare people away. You should be accommodating and approachable. When your fans upload interesting content, like and repost if it is positive. Be supportive, and people will turn to appreciate you. Most musicians on Tik Tok and other social media platforms appear to be difficult and hard to approach. Some of them prefer to maintain a proper distance from their audience rather than associating with them. As an artist, you should not allow pride to lead you, even though popular musicians and producers have a different perspective on their audience. You should come differently. This action can create a secret success route for you. However, your prestige is essential. While you relate with your audience, limit your conversation to a certain level.

9. Never forget your intentions

On this platform, you may decide to digress from your initial type of content, but this might be dangerous for upcoming musicians, as you can lose a great number of your fans. Influencers and top musicians are coming out with engaging challenges just to capture people's interest. If you are not careful enough, you might join the trend and forget your primary intention on Tik Tok. Whatever you do on the platform, always have this in the back of your mind; your music is the major priority that brought you to the platform. While participating in any challenge, recreate it in a form that it will promote your music in return. Creativity is all that is required. The more you promote yourself the more attention you will get from fans. When you forget your intentions, you may find it hard to move an inch in terms of your musical dreams. Your intentions should reflect in your daily post as well. You can just create your everyday post to inform people that you are musically endowed. Some of your videos might just be for your brand name promotion. When your name is common among your audience, just bear in mind that your success is closer than expected. Good intentions towards your career will turn out to stand as a source of blessing to you. Tik Tok audience is meant to believe any video content presented before them. All that is required is an engaging video to start with.

10. Organize a Tik Tok challenge for your new music:

Tik Tok challenges have created a great impact on top brands in the social media world. Before the platform came into the limelight, influencers, and artists in other social media platforms have been organizing challenges for their audience. However, Tik Tok came with a different perspective on social media challenges. Most challenges organized on it tend to go viral. Hence, you should consider a Tik Tok challenge for your new music. A challenge can enlighten people to develop an interest in your music. To create a challenge that will go viral, you will have to adhere strictly to steps and procedures.

- **Watch some viral challenges organized by other musicians:**

  Before you will consider organizing a challenge, you should do proper research to discover the idea behind their challenge. You can select musicians that gained their fame via Tik Tok challenge and study their success route. Upon arriving on the Tik Tok page, you should follow musicians like @postmalone, @panicatthedisco @sleepingwithsiren, and many others. You can easily discover the concept behind their video, and apply the same to your videos.

- **Create an easy challenge:**

  Never create a difficult challenge, as most people will decline their interest. Endeavor to keep your Tik Tok challenge simple and engaging. Tik Tok users prefer to participate in challenges that require fewer skills to do.

- **Throw the challenge open for all:**

  You don't have to be selective when it comes to your audience. Since you are new in the game, you should allow everyone to participate. Some Tik Tok users whom you might think show less interest may turn out to become your top fans.

- **Collaborate with top influencers:**

  Even though it may require a price, you should see it as an investment, because you will enjoy the outcome alone. Find Tik Tok influencers that have contributed to the success of various challenges and work with them. You never can tell, if that will become your road towards fame and recognition. Influencers will contribute towards the success of your challenge by encouraging their audience to participate in the challenge. These influencers will tend to participate in the challenge as well. You may become surprised with traffic and attention coming from different people to your Tik Tok account.

List of ten popular challenges on TikTok you should check out

Tik Tok is bigger than you are seeing it. Different challenges organized by musicians and top brands have exposed the viral abilities of the platform. Most musicians have developed the habit of using TikTok to make their music go viral. You can check out these popular challenges and use them as a reference point.

- **#Blindinglights Challenge**:

  Weekend released blinding lights in 2019, and many people fell in love with the song. Tik Tok users decide to turn the song into a dance challenge. The blinding light challenge gained a lot of attention and it got over 300 million views from several TikTok users. You can study the challenge and apply some of your observations in your challenge.

- **#Fliptheswitch Challenge**:

  This challenge attracted the attention of prominent people like Senator Elizabeth Warren and many others. It's a dance challenge organized to promote Drake's song "Non-Stop". The challenge got over 600 million views, and a lot of TikTok users participated actively in this challenge. The challenge allows two people to participate in it. One person will appear to be dancing while the other person is standing, after a while, they will flip the switch off during which they will then swap their clothes and standing position, before switching back the light. You can check out this challenge on TikTok.

- **#Updown Challenge:**

This type of challenge started like a dance challenge whereby TikTok users are required to do the up-down dance with family members. However, some TikTok users decide to add creativity to the challenge by coming different. This challenge gained over 50 million views from TikTokers, you can learn a lot from this challenge.

- **#Savage Challenge:**

This challenge became so popular after Mega Thee Stallion dropped her song "savage". Most people on Tik Tok copied the choreography of the song and started a challenge with it. The challenge became one of the most successful challenges ever organized in Tik Tok. It gained over 670 million views.

- **#renegeda Challenge:**

This challenge was started with a hard dance from a 14-year-old Tik Tok user named Jalaiah Harmon. She decides to create the dance out of

K Camp's song titled "Lottery" and the challenge turns out to gain a lot of attention from people.

- **#Celeblookalike Challenge:**

  This challenge only requires Tik Tok users to compare themselves with their look-alike celebrities. This challenge got more than 100 million views within a short space of time.

- **#Firstmovelastmove Challenge:**

  This challenge is all about dance. Two people are meant to dance, whereby the second person uses the first person's last move as his/her first move.

- **#Supalonely dance:** This dance gained a lot of attention from several people. The dance came with a popular trend and became one of the hottest trends on TikTok. It gained more than 200 million views within a short time.

- **#Canttouchthis Challenge:**

  Tik Tok users embraced this challenge with Macarena dance. However, if you are not familiar with this dance, then you should not consider organizing a challenge like this.

- **#Toosieslide Challenge:**

  Michael Jackson's moonwalk is the brain behind

this challenge. Tik Tok users decide to create the dance in this format "when the right foot is up, left foot will slide, and when the left foot is up, the right foot will slide"

11. Use Hashtags:

Apart from Instagram, Tik Tok also enables hashtag marketing. You can use a lot of popular trending hashtags to grow your audience. Since people love dancing, singing, and other related fun activities, you can use hashtags like #dance, #meme #music and a lot more are very popular on TikTok. Using the right hashtags on Tik Tik will expose your music to these benefits;

- **Attracts more exposure and views**:

  Tik Tok users are always busy searching for the right video to fit their mood, and most of them are younger people. If your video is engaging and you use the right hashtag to upload your video, you will get a lot of reaction within a short time. One good feature of using hashtags is that you can gain popularity faster than you expect.

- **Promotes your Tik Tok account**:

  Hashtags do not only boost your videos to top search, but your account will gain more followers in return. Once your video starts to gain reactions from different people, you will experience a lot of follow-back from the people as well, Most audiences that fell in love with your video will likely follow your account to keep up to date with your regular uploads.

- **Pushes your music**:

  A hashtag will give your music an unexpected boost. You might be surprised when you see your music trending outside TikTok. Most people that visit your handle will prefer to learn more about your previous songs. You might be lucky enough to gain quick fame through this strategy.

Ways to discover the right Hashtag for your music video

The question you may be asking is how to discover the right hashtags to use. This might be difficult if you are new to Tik Tok, but you might go through people's videos and discover a lot from them. Good Tik Tok users always attach some popular hashtags on their videos. You can discover some trending hashtags from them, or you can search for hashtags and see the popular ones. However, you should not panic about finding the right hashtags for your video, as this approach will save the situation;

- **Use the Tik Tok tool:**

  Your music genre does not determine the type of hashtag to use because almost everybody loves music. Therefore, search for available TikTok tools and discover more popular hashtags.

- **Learn from popular posts:**

  You can see several videos on the Tik Tok home page, and you can also see the Hashtags used to boost the visibility of such videos. Watch the video to discover the content and compare how the video relates to the hashtags. You can use the same hashtags for your video as well.

- **Follow music influencers:**

  There are a lot of music influencers on Instagram. Following them will give you an insight into the type of hashtags they use frequently. Watch how they create their videos to match with the hashtag and do the same thing to your post. Some of these influencers use hashtags that people hardly discover. You can join the influencers and use their hashtags on your post as well.

- **Search for hashtags:**

  You can search for hashtags using the search icon. Tik Tok will rank the available hashtags based on the number of posts made with them.

Best Tool for Tik Tok Hashtag

When it comes to the Tik Tok hashtag, you have to use some generators to gain access to more useful hashtags. Some of these tools will help you to discover hashtags faster;

- **All Hashtags**:

  This type of hashtag generator is one of the best hashtag generation tools you can ever use. All that is required from you is one keyword and the tool will generate the rest for you. It operates as an automated system. It tends to display all the trending hashtags that relate to your post, then you will have to select the suitable hashtags that march with your post and add up. One amazing feature of this tool is that it tends to filter your post based on your interest with its three options feature.

- **Seekmetrics**:

  This tool helps Tik Tok users to find suitable hashtags for their post. The tool only requires a keyword from you, and then it will proceed to display other hashtags that you can easily copy and paste in your post. This tool also outlines your performance with its metrics in comparative features.

- **Hashtag generating websites**:

  A lot of websites tend to help Tik Tok users generate hashtags for their upload. You will have to make sure that the website is unique before investing your time on them. Websites like tiktokhashtags.com will only require a keyword from you, then it will generate several hashtags related to your keyword. Also, influencermarketinghub.com/tiktok-hashtag-generator/ can help you with a lot of hashtags.

Most Popular Hashtags commonly used on Tik Tok

Some of Tik Tok hashtags have become so popular that people use it so often to upload their every post. Since the platform consists of vibrant young people, some of these popular hashtags have to represent what could be on their minds. You will have to bear in mind that your Hashtag choice has to represent your music content. Below is the list of 50 popular hashtags on Tik Tok;

1. #Musically

2. #comedy

3. #memes

4. #followforfollowback

5. #happy

6. #Fun

7. #love

8. #Lol

9. #followme

10. #tiktok

11. #Likeforfollow

12. #girl

13. #cute

14. #Funny

15. #repost

16. #picoftheday

17. #repost4follow

18. #Summer

19. #me

20. #Black

21. #funnyvideos

22. #work

23. #Lifestyle

24. #blackandwhite

25. #tbt

26. #selfie

27. #dance

28. #video

29. #like4like

30. #amazing

31. #sky

32. #follow

33. #fitness

34. #yummy

35. #pink

36. #fashion

37. #darkmemes

38. #ootd

39. #dog

40. #cat

41. #photooftheday

42. #nature

43. #christmas

44. #nyc

45. #viral

46. #photography

47. #talk

48. #myvoice

49. #naturalbeauty

50. #music

How Lil Nas gained his Fame from Tik Tok

Lil Nas X was born in Georgia on April 9, 1999. His real name is Montero Lamar Hills. He decided to change his stage name to Lil Nas X as a tribute to Nas. He attended the Lithia Spring High School and graduated in 2017, after which he enrolled in the University of West Georgia. However, he dropped out of university after a year to pursue a music career. Lil Nas X admitted that he spent a lot of time on the internet during his earlier age just to promote his meme. During an interview with Rolling Stone, he revealed, "I was doing Facebook comedy videos, and then moved to Instagram, and then to Twitter, where I really was a master. That was the first place where I could go viral." He started writing songs in his closet. In December 2018, he dropped his single hit "Old Town Road" where he started to gain attention from people. In February 2019, he decided to upload the song on his Tik Tok account, and that was the beginning of his journey to fame. He started a meme to promote the song on Tik Tok. Within a couple of months, the meme got millions of reactions from Tik Tok users. In July 2019, Tik Tok US general manager congratulated Lil Nas X on his success on their platform. While addressing the press, he revealed: "It's been incredible to watch Old Town Road grow from its start on Tik Tok in February, as the backbone of an accessible and engaging meme that generated millions of creations and billions of view, to a record-breaking smash hit that has all walks of life listening on repeat." The song lasted for 17 weeks on the billboard hot 100.

Lessons from the success of Lil Nas X to upcoming musicians

From the success story of Lil Nas X, you can figure out that every musician needs to be unique and different from the crowd. All that is required is just one hit track, and you will be on your road to success. Lil Nas X was dedicated, and he used his previous meme creation skills to boost his popular song. Despite his new choice of life to become a musician, he never forgot his old creative way of approaching the audience. From this success story, you should be able to extract the following points;

- **Powerful lyric is the key**: Lil Nas X wouldn't have gone that far if his lyrics were poor. If you have listened to his popular song, 'Old Town Road', you will discover that he worked extra hard to put the lyrics together. Even if you prefer to work with other songwriters, always define your intentions and make it unique and engaging. Review your lyrics before taking it into the studio.

- **Hard work pays**: No man ever becomes a billionaire by mistake. A lot of hard work and dedication is required to achieve success. As an artist, you should focus on your career more than anything else. Lil Nas X worked hard to get his song trending on every platform. You can do the same to your song as well.

- **Avoid distractions**: Distractions can kill big dreams. Imagine having a lot of distractions around you, your output will always be discouraging and poor. Lil Nas X discovered that his university education will distract his music career, so he quickly dropped out of school to pursue his career. However, this does not mean that you should drop out of school like Lil Nas, but if any activity tends to disrupt your activities, you should disengage yourself from such activities before it ruins your career.

- **Add creativity to your Tik Tok uploads**: Lil Nas was good at this, he used the meme to draw people's attention to his new track. You should give this a trial by changing the way you upload your videos. Make it look attractive and interesting.

- **Be positive**: Positive minds can always attain any height. Don't look at your limitation, look above your limitation, and discover bigger dreams.

MUSIC PROMOTION ON YOUTUBE

YouTube is the biggest platform for musicians. The platform tends to stream music more than any other platform. YouTube has about 85% of young age demographics, and younger people love to watch music videos a lot. As a musician, your music must be on this platform and if you are yet to create an account, you should consider giving it a trial. On YouTube, your major concern should be subscribers and views. You can urge your followers on other platforms to visit your channel and subscribe for more videos. However, your success on this platform must be channeled to this creative approach;

1. **Create an engaging channel for your music**

    The face of your YouTube channel will determine

if people will turn out to subscribe to it. Instead of adding a boring picture on your channel, why not try an avatar or a creative design that defines your music genre. Also, create a playlist to arrange your content in order. Don't forget to link your profile with your website, and other social media platforms. This linkage will give your YouTube subscribers access to your other social media platforms. Design an attractive channel banner to attract more visitors.

2. Work with other YouTubers

Just like Tik Tok and Instagram, YouTube has influencers. Some creators have worked hard to gain millions of subscribers, and they create room to promote upcoming musicians. You should look out for these types of people and network with them. To connect with them is not that difficult, you will just have to send them a direct message. But before messaging them, subscribe to their channel and stay active in the comment section of their daily upload. You can easily gain their attention through this creative approach.

3. Upload consistently:

Consistent uploads are necessary, as your fans are always looking out for something to watch on this platform. You should always bear in mind that youtube is all about videos, and people storm the platform just to watch videos. Therefore, give them something to watch. You can recreate your music video in another creative way and upload it. Your every upload must not appear as new music. You can come out with something different at all times.

4. **YouTube SEO can change the face of your channel**:

SEO simply means, 'Search Engine Optimization'. YouTube allows you to write about a 5000-word description of the video content. You ought to add creative writing to this description section. YouTube ranks videos based on their SEO, and when you use the perfect SEO to upload on your videos, you will discover a huge difference on your channel. In writing SEO, you should include relevant keywords from a regular youtube search to boost your chances of appearing in the top search. The title of your video has to reflect your description. Try to keep it short and relevant. When people are searching for topics related to your song, YouTube will push your videos to them. Tags are also another element that you should include in your video description. Your tags should begin with hashtags (#). Your tags must be relevant.

5. Check out other music channels on YouTube:

There are several music channels on YouTube channels that music artists neglect to check out. You shouldn't be like everybody. Visit every music channel within your reach and learn from them. You may be lucky enough to connect with prominent musicians who may give your channel a boost. Your major target should always be on growing your subscribers and you should work extra hard to achieve this. The best way of getting quicker fame is to find a music channel on YouTube that uploads the same music genre as yours. All that is required from you is active participation in every video upload. You can drop one relevant comment and wait for people's reactions. Let's take, for example, if you are a rapper, you should subscribe to every artist who does a similar music genre with you.

6. Don't Joke with Trends

In our world today, anything can become a trend, and you should consider utilizing any trend to push your music career. As an artist, you should be creative enough to convert every trend into engaging music content. In case you don't know, millions of Youtubers storm the platform in search of videos that relate to such trends. All you're required to do is to boost your channel with just one amazing, trendy video. People will subscribe to your channel after watching the video.

7. **Do proper research on your keywords before usage:**

YouTube cannot discover keywords mentioned in your videos, you will still have to make out time and find some relevant keywords yourself. Finding the perfect keyword words for your videos may be challenging and difficult to achieve. However, you can discover the right keywords when you use a ranking tool such as 'Rank Tracker'. This keyword discovery tool allows you to access the closet keywords related to your topic. Once you download the software on your Windows or Mac OS. Launch immediately and discover the deepest keyword you could ever imagine. keywords are more powerful than people see it. The success of most viral content relates to keywords. Since YouTube is the second most used search engine, you should not deny your videos with relevant keywords in the descriptive section. When your post appears on the top search, you can always gain more subscribers and views from YouTubers. No matter how good your video content might appear, unrelated keywords can hide your videos behind the poorly organized video. Apart from referring your fans from other platforms to navigate to your youtube channel and subscribe, YouTube search engine will attract more audiences to you with the right keywords.

8. Use YouTube analytics to monitor your video:

YouTube has analytics that allows creators to monitor the growth of their channel and video content. Whenever a viewer checked in, youtube analytics will notify you where you gained your view from, their age demographics, how long they spent watching your video, and more. With this information, you will discover where your major audience is coming from, and you can always make your videos relate well with them. If the time they spend watching your videos is short, consider doing a better video. As an artist, you should make music videos that define your lyrics. And the graphics should be high quality and attractive. You can hire potential video-makers to give you the best quality. Also, your analytics will give you an insight into the related keywords that enabled people to gain access to your videos. You can use this method to adjust your video description.

9. Change the name of your video before uploading:

There is a need to rename your video before uploading it. Most people will think that this action is not necessary. However, Youtube may optimize the original name of the video while ranking search results. You can rename your video to define the content of the video. For instance, if your video is all about cars, you can use a car-related topic to rename your video. If the original name of the video is file.mp4, you should rename it to future-cars.mp4 or any other relevant keyword that relates to cars. The naming of your video (if not a music video) should draw the reader in. Vague video titles will limit your video success.

10. Create mobile-friendly videos:

Most YouTubers prefer to grace the platform with their mobile smartphones. So you should keep your uploads in a mobile-friendly format. Your effort to drive more traffic on your content depends highly on the nature of your videos. However, some Youtubers still prefer to watch videos using their computers; therefore, you should endeavor to organize a good management system to accommodate all your viewers.

How Justin Bieber became popular on YouTube

Justin Bieber was born in Ontario on March 14th, 1994. He was raised by a single mother Pattie Mallette. His dad, Jeremy Bieber, left Mallette while Bieber was 13 months old. Bieber grew up without a close relationship with his dad. In his earlier stages, Bieber developed an interest in music, and he learned how to play piano, guitar, trumpet, and drum. Bieber grew up playing guitar on the street. As a little boy, he loves sports as well as music. His mother supported his music career more than his sports dreams. While in high school, Bieber participated in a local singing competition held in Strafford. During the competition, he performed Neyo's Hit Track titled 'So sick'. His performance wowed the organizer of the competition, and he won the second position. Mallette recorded his performance and uploaded the video on youtube for her family and friends to watch. After that, she kept on uploading videos of Justin covering most RnB popular songs on YouTube. Due to her consistent upload, the formal marketing executive of So So Def Records, Scooter Braun, was able to discover Justin in 2007. It happened accidentally, he was searching for a different musician when he clicked on Bieber's video. The rest became a story. Justin is forever, grateful to his mum, youtube, and Scooter Braun.

Observation from Justin Bieber's success

As a good observer, you should be able to point out the major moves behind the success of Bieber. However, your observation should tally with these points;

1. **Determined**:

   Despite the difficulty faced by Justin during his earlier age, he never allowed his vision to go blur. Through the help of his mother, he gained attention from people, and he was fortunate enough to get the needful attention that leads to his success. Your connection may not come like Justin Bieber's own, but if your music content is good, you can easily win the heart of many people.

2. **Bieber had a different view on music**:

   Despite his young age, Bieber showed interest in several musical instruments, and he was able to play Drum, guitar, piano, and trumpet. This action has shown that Bieber had a great passion for music. As a musician, you should develop an interest in musical instruments as well. Don't misunderstand this statement, you can still become a musician without having any knowledge on the instrument, but your ability to develop skills on different musical instruments will give you a step above your competitors. You can always gain more attention when you develop good skills on several musical instruments. At least, you will have something to offer your audience per day.

3. Consistent upload:

Bieber's mum was consistent with the video uploads, and she never gave up on her son. Justin's video was discovered because of his mother's effort to get her son to the top. YouTubers love to watch a lot of engaging videos, so Mallette saw that as an opportunity, and today, her son is famous. You can do a lot of work on your videos and success will become your priority.

TRILLER

Triller App was created in July 2015 by David Leiberman and Sammy Rubin. David emphasized on his Linkedin account that the app was created on his birthday as a music editing app with amazing auto-editing properties. The app is powered with AI features which enables the app to auto edit videos for creators. The platform has over 10 million active monthly users with over 500 million users across all social media platforms. Most popular musicians grace this platform to share their music content with fans. Also, the Triller app has made it possible for video creators to share their videos on several platforms without much stress. Since people are embracing the platform because of its AI auto video editing features, the Triller app decides to use the AI features as its unique marketing point. The auto-editing features collect the best part of a video and merge it together to create an engaging music video. As a result of this, most musicians prefer this platform to other social media platforms. Before you upload your videos on this platform, you should note the following;

1. **Triller Videos must be engaging**:

   The platform works better for hip-hop musicians who create a lot of interesting videos. Therefore, your ability to engage an audience is necessary on this platform. What this implies is that when you create unprofessional music videos, your chances will be limited.

2. **Fan's pays more attention to fun**:

   Most fans on this platform appreciate creative videos with fun attributes. For instance, when @kyreedatsme decided to upload videos doing weird but entertaining videos, his view count began to rise. When he first started, his videos were minimal in terms of entertainment which heavily affected the video view count. The example above is a true definition of fans' reaction to funny videos. As an artist, you can use this strategy as your unique selling point on this platform.

3. **Triller audience loves unique creators**:

   If you are not a creative musician, this platform may not work well for you. As your audience is always looking up to you for something different and new.

How to build a better relationship with your audience on Triller

Followers on different social media platforms almost have the same thing in common. They love to get feedback from you. As a musician that wants to build huge success on this platform, you should consider using this creative approach.

1. **Follow back your fans**:

    You might see this as a stressful approach, however, it will attract more people who are desperately looking for a follow back. You can easily discover engaging content made by a fan and appreciate their effort. You may not follow back all your fans but try to follow back at least 10% of your audience. This action will enable you to establish a better relationship with your audience. However, your ability to follow back your fans highly depends on their number. If your audience is tremendously large, you may capitalize on your effort on fans that are always active on your every post.

2. Repost their contents:

When you repost their content, you are indirectly giving them a boost. Triller audiences love musicians that are supportive. You will be surprised by the tremendous feedback you will get from them. However, before reposting content created by your fans, you will have to put a lot into consideration. Some content may tend to affect people's life negatively, and reposting such content on your account may change the mindset of your audience. Therefore, preview the video content and make sure that it deserves a repost from you before acting. Apart from reposting the content within the triller app, you can also share the content with your other social media handles.

3. Like and comment on their post:

Social media platforms have made it possible for people to appreciate creators' effort with comments and likes. In case you don't know, people value your comments and likes. It encourages them to create more content related to that post. You can use this catchy method to maintain a good relationship with them. You can watch their reaction when you comment on their post and determine your next line of action. If your audience is large, you may appreciate their content at random. However, no one will penalize you for not commenting on people's posts, but it will likely make you more influential.

4. **Join every popular challenge**:

Generally, people love to watch trends, and Triller app is a platform where challenges are common practice. Your success on this platform depends on how active you are, with the latest development. During a challenge, musicians and video creators embrace this platform to share their creative idea on the trend. You should participate actively and do the necessary follow up. A known musician may decide to come up with a new challenge just to promote his/ her album or single. You can partake in many challenges and win the heart of people. One important approach that people neglect on every social media platform is their ability to win the heart of people with trends. No matter how bad you are in dancing, the Triller app can get it ready for your audience to see. Most challenges usually beckon on dance, so you are required to develop your dancing skills and get ready to showcase your talent to any trending challenge on this platform. If you check most famous musicians of different social media platforms, they are always active on most trending challenges, as that is the gateway to their success,

Best challenges to participate in Triller

When it comes to challenges, the triller app has a lot of them. Just like Tik Tok, challenges on triller are made popular with hashtags. You can discover the current trending songs with a certain keyword. However, musicians on Triller prefer to engage their audience with mostly dance challenge videos. Artists like Rae Sremmurd used a thriller dance video to boost his new song on Instagram. You can create a similar trend with your music video and push it to the top. Your ability to participate actively in challenges organized in the platform will determine your success. There are two popular challenges on Triller app and they include;

1. **Dance challenge**:

   This type of challenge is all about dance. You will recreate a special dancing skill to gain more attention from people. Before you will proceed to create your unique dance video, watch already trending videos and come out with something different and unique.

2. **Lip sync challenge**:

   This challenge will enable you to understand the brain behind professional music video making. On this challenge, participants are expected to record themselves moving their lips to synchronize with the lyrics on the background music. Therefore, before you participate in this challenge, you ought to do research on the song in question and rehearse the lyrics before recording yourself in action. Preparing before participating in the challenge will give your video a boost.

How to use Triller app

The software is made available to suit different devices (mostly suitable mobile devices), and it is only compatible with android and apple OS. However, if you have yet to download the software on your mobile devices, you should follow these procedures;

1. **Visit your play store to download the app:** This app is designed for mobile usage alone. You can proceed to obtain the app from google play store or apple store and begin your journey to fame.

2. **Launch the app:** Once installed on your mobile, launch the app to see the available features, and to ensure that you downloaded the right version for your device. Immediately you land at the first interface of the app, you will discover a home icon, a search icon, a "+" icon, a notification icon, and last a profile icon. You also discover a series of creative videos made available by different content creators.

3. **Signing up on Triller:** On the first interface, you will discover a profile icon at the right bottom of the video. Navigate to that icon and you will navigate to the sign-in page. The app allows you to sign up with Facebook, Instagram, Twitter, email, or phone number. You will have to select any suitable sign-in method and proceed. When you select any of these signup methods, the Triller app will expect you to verify your account before proceeding. You can navigate to the inbox of the selected sign up method and obtain the signup code. Once you enter the code, the triller app will access it before allowing you to choose your username. After that, then your profile is ready for usage. You can proceed to edit your profile by selecting the "edit profile" icon. On this page, you add every account that you wish to connect with your triller account, you can make the account private if you want. But people won't be able to find your videos unless you give them access to it. So it's advisable not to use this option. When you are done with this edit, return to your home page and follow a couple of users.

4. **Build your friend zone:** Since you're new on this platform, you ought to follow some people to learn more about the video contents people post on triller. The platform recommends following some popular people. Triller will also allow you

to find friends from your Facebook, Instagram, and other platforms. You can also send a direct message to friends by using the message icon which is similar to Instagram Dm.

5. **Tapping on the home icon:** When you tap on this icon, you will navigate to your home page, where you will discover a series of videos uploaded by people you followed. You can scroll and select any video of your choice.

6. **Tapping on the search icon:** The search icon will activate the search button which allows you to find your desired videos. However, if you are not too sure of the search video, you can select a category under the search button and the triller app will filter the search result to contain only the selected category.

7. **Tapping on the notification icon:** This icon will allow you to access all the activities that happen within your account. Whenever you get a new follower, the triller app will notify you through this icon.

8. **Tapping on the "+" icon:** When you tap this icon, it will navigate you to a page whereby you can create a music video or a vlog. When you select the music video, it will navigate you to the next page where you can access the trending

music features, Spotify, and my music icon. On the page, you can select a song from the list of songs provided by the platform. You can tap on the left side of the screen to preview the song, or you can select the song by tapping directly on the song track. You can select your choice of music and proceed. At this point, you ought to know this; the feature icon represents the top hit songs selected by the triller app just to showcase the current trend. The new music icon allows you to upload a song from your iTunes library to your Triller account. Spotify allows you to access music uploads on its platform. There is a search button on top of the feature and a new music icon. You can use this button to find your desired song on the platform. When you select a song, it will navigate you to the next page.

9. **Trim the audio**: This page will allow you to select the duration and the part of the song you want to use. The duration has to range from 15 seconds to 30 seconds. However, you should try to keep your video at 15 seconds or less.

10. **Start recording**: When you are done, tap the film icon on top. It will demand access to your camera. At this point, you should allow the triller app to gain access to your camera. If you have recorded the video before now, tap on the gallery icon to upload the video from your

gallery. But if you prefer to record directly on your phone, tap on the camera icon, and the video will count down from 3,2 1, and then will start to record. During the recording, you can zone in and out to capture the scene very well. On the right side, you can adjust your camera to suit your recording.

11. **Auto editing features**: All that is required from you is to press shuffle and the app will auto edit your video, however, you can go ahead and edit the video yourself.

12. **Add a description**: Most people neglect this section, and it happens to be that the description section is the most important section on every video upload. Your videos will gain attention if you use the right keyword to upload them.

13. **Choose a Category**: Here, you will have to choose a category based on the type of video you just made. The categories on the triller app include; comedy, dance, fashion/beauty, food, lifestyle/travel, music, sports, workout/fitness. You can set the video as private (which is not advisable, unless for some reason) and tag your location.

14. **Share on other platforms**: Once you are done with your upload, the triller app allows you to share your video on other platforms like

Facebook, Instagram, Twitter, Youtube or you can tap the 'more icon' to discover other social media handles. You can download the video and save it in your gallery. On the bottom right of your screen, the triller app will display the progress of your download, and once you are done, you will receive a **notification.**

FACEBOOK

Facebook stands as a top social media platform with billions of users. This platform makes it possible for musicians to boost their music videos with ads. According to statista.com, Facebook has about 1.69 billion users in 2020. These massive users are supportive and ready to embrace new and interesting content. You can use Facebook to grow your fan base. Before posting any content on Facebook, you should bear in mind that most users are also active on their social media platforms such as Youtube, TikTok, Instagram, Twitter, and many others. Therefore, you can also encourage your users to follow your other social media handle. Your success on Facebook depends on the following;

1. **Create a Facebook page**: Before anything else, you should create a page using your brand name and get the page active. You can invite your

friends to follow your page, and ask them to invite their friends as well.

2. **Upload contents on your page**: You should keep your page active with contents to keep your fan base active.

3. **Run Facebook ads to promote your page:** You should run facebook ads to gain more followers and views. People are desperately searching for content to view on this platform. You should utilize this opportunity and make your content go viral.

4. **Work with influencers**: You can easily win the heart of many music influencers on this platform and their pay is not that high when compared with music influencers in other platforms.

A Successful music influencer, Kyree, and his view on how musicians can excel through social media platforms

Kyree is a well-known music influencer, who has helped hundreds of musicians gain their fame within a while. He has worked with Lil Tecca, Yo Gotti, and many others. The music influencer has decided to dish out the best marketing strategy on Instagram for musicians and producers. From his observation, he emphasized more on the following marketing strategies;

1. Hashtag

The hashtag is by far, one of the best marketing strategies to deploy for a successful campaign. Kyree stated that hashtags help with people looking for a related hashtag to discover your post, and this action will help your post to receive more likes and boost the visibility of your page. He also emphasized more on how to verify if your Instagram hashtag is getting attention. While explaining his view on this, he stated that when you have a business profile, which is compulsory for every artist, that you should check your insights and discover if the used hashtags are actually driving people's attention to your page. From his point of view, you will discover that your Instagram can always be better when you use hashtags to make your post available for several audiences.

2. Call to action:

Kyree urged musicians to use this strategy often, as it has helped several artists gain their fame on Instagram. On this note, he said that while uploading a post on your Instagram, you should endeavor to think of a call to action or develop a strategy that is going to make your viewers impressed and also help them to relate well with the caption. The reason why Kyree emphasized more on captions is that most musicians ignore uploading their posts with suitable captions. From this point, you will observe that there is a need to come up with a creative caption to keep your audience engaged. You can make the caption look like a question or something that will motivate your audience to engage with your post.

3. **Instagram Live:**

Kyree Hollis shares his view on Instagram live, he stated that he supports musicians to connect other artists on their live chat because when they are connected together, their followers will mix together. Imagine when you go live with a popular musician with millions of followers; your following will grow after the live chat. Instagram live has boosted the potentials of many known musicians such as Tory Lanez, Teddy Riley, and many others.

TWITCH

Twitch was designed specifically for online video streaming. Usually, video content on this platform can surface through video demand or live video. The platform was created in 2011 and it grew rapidly with a couple of years. Musicians are navigating to this platform as its getting maximum attention from the public. Twitch is owned by Amazon and the platform focus more on prerecorded gameplay and broadcast.

How Twitch works

Twitch is mainly for sharing videos for viewing. Twitch makes its money through advertisement and membership monthly subscription. Advertisers are mostly top gaming companies, game developers, and many other potential companies. In this platform, you can decide to become a turbo membership to gain access to ad-free videos on twitch. The platform accepts PayPal donations as well. However, the monthly subscription costs $8.99. Therefore every upcoming artist that wish to gain their fame via twitch will have to adhere strictly to this twitch working procedure;

- **Registration section**: Twitch allows its users to gain access to it via the mobile app or desktop. However, you can access it on the mobile by downloading from google play store or apple store. Sign up and confirm your mobile number.

- **Access twitch videos**: Once you confirm your sign up method, proceed to access other people's videos. You can upload yours to gain peoples' attention faster.

How to make money from Twitch

Most musicians on twitch make their money through partnership programs. They apply for partnership with Twitch and earn their share from the advert coming in from top brands and gaming companies. However, before you will consider making a partnership with Twitch, you ought to build your following and stand a better chance to make more money on twitch. Also, twitch partners must be active in streaming relevant content for their users. Before becoming a twitch partner, you ought to complete your partnership achievement before anything else. Note that your music contents must meet up with twitch's terms and conditions. Therefore, review the terms and conditions before joining their partnership programs. You can monetize your twitch account through any these methods;

1. **Bit**: Bit is twitch's digital currency, and the platform can go to any length just to promote their digital currency. You can grab this opportunity and give a boost to their currency.

2. **Streamloots**: Streamloots allow viewers to gain access to a card and each card has a prize attached to it.

3. **Sponsorship**: This monetization method is common in twitch. You can also get a gift from the sponsor in the long run. You can charge brands to add their content to your music videos and vlogs. However, your following will determine if you will get the attention of top brands.

Apart from these three methods, there are other ways to monetize your twitch account. However, you will discover them as time goes on.

The reason why you should consider using Twitch more often as a musician

Twitch Platform is one of the best platforms for Livestream videos because your viewers will be required to subscribe to your Twitch's account, just to watch your videos. Also, you can receive donations from your viewers as well. Hence, you can have more fun on Twitch when you increase your fan base. Building a community on this platform is also another means of getting more attention from its users. Twitch users prefer to join a community based on their interest in a certain category. As a musician, you should consider utilizing this opportunity to build your audience even from zero.

How Twitch works for Musicians and Producers

Twitch platform enables musicians to communicate effectively with their audience. Live streaming can unite musicians and their fan base closely even more than their regular posts. Since streaming on Twitch is different from other social media platforms, every musician should consider joining this platform because;

1. **Music category is still open for fresh music:** Just like YouTube and other top social media platforms, whereby musicians compete among themselves just to stay at the top, Twitch is different. You can take the lead easily on this platform when you deploy a creative strategy.

2. **Twitch shows more concern on Music Category:** Previously, Twitch focused on other

categories. However, the platform has changed its focus toward the music category. Twitch now features music content on its home page. Since they are consistent with this action, your music can easily gain up to 5000 concurrent views within a short time. However, popular music streamers on Twitch achieve an average of 200 to 300 views per video. To show their full support for music, Twitch came up with a karaoke game idea known as Twitch sing. Twitch sing allows musicians to participate in their fan/creator conferences which normally come as the American Idol Singing Competition. A winner of this challenge will go home $20,000 cash price and a single release with Columbia records.

3. **You don't need to partner with brands or depend on ads to monetize your Twitch:** Twitch is a platform that deserves your time as an upcoming musician because the platform pays musicians directly from their viewers. If you can engage better with your fans on live video, then open a play request and keep them engaged. When they watch you on the Livestream, they will feel closely attached to your community. Your fan base can easily expand and most fans will subscribe and donate to your channel. You can also monetize your Twitch account via virtual currency and Twitch channel subscription.

However, you must reach a certain benchmark to earn from the above-listed methods.

4. **Livestreaming on Twitch is easier to accomplish:** Live Streaming videos on social media platforms do not undergo proper edits just like your regular post. Since it does not require filters and a perfect touch to impress the audience, you can use this often to engage your Twitch fan base.

5. **Monetization comes from what you love doing:** Your audience will likely subscribe to your Twitch account if your videos impress them. Donations from your audience can easily push your music to the top list.

6. **Twitch community is big:** People come together on this platform to share related content. You should consider joining a particular community, or create one to engage your audience.

MUSIC DISTRIBUTION

Apart from sharing your music on several social media platforms, some platforms stand as the best distribution channel for musicians. Some of these channels include;

Spotify

Spotify was developed by a Swedish music provider in 2008. Musicians use this platform a lot to stream their music. Its users can find their favorite artists through the search category. The search category includes artist name, genre, or album. Spotify is available in Europe, New Zealand, Australia, America, and some parts of Asia and Africa.

How Spotify works for musicians

Uploading music on Spotify may become a challenging task for upcoming musicians. However, if you're signed to a music label, you won't have much problem as your label will upload your music to Spotify. An Independent musician can still take the lead and work with a distributor to get your music to the platform. Also, you should note that Spotify partnered with companies who can license and distribute your music on its platform.

You should note that Spotify is open for musicians to express themselves through positive music content. In a situation whereby the musician uploads illegal or hateful content, Spotify can easily take down the song.

What is Spotify Playlisting?

Spotify playlist contains lists of songs saved for a later date. Spotify users prefer to arrange their playlists to separate their favorite music from the general platform. Spotify has its official playlist and individuals can create their playlist as well. Musicians can use Spotify playlisting as their unique marketing strategy. Playlist in Spotify can be established in two different ways;

1. **Official Spotify Playlisting**: Official playlisting is created by the Spotify curated team to support their users arrange the favorite music together. The platform places these playlists in a position where every user can access them. However, some personal playlists may tend to appear in the

position with these official playlists. Therefore the position of playlists on the app will be determined by the Spotify Curation team.

2. **Personal Spotify Playlisting**: Users of this platform can create their playlists. Most musicians and bloggers make their playlist in order to carry their audience along. You can create this type of playlist to share with heavy Spotify users. If your playlists are too engaging, Spotify may feature your playlist on its platform, and this action will boost your chances of increasing your fan base.

How Playlisting helps Musicians to grow their fan base and gain more streams

Spotify playlisting helps artists to grow their fan base and gain more streams as well. Playlists help musicians grow their fan base by having their songs featured amongst other genre related songs and artists. Music lovers on Spotify spend countless hours listening to playlists. . As an artist, you should consider submitting your song to playlist curators for playlisting. A music industry analyst, Mark Mulligan, once emphasized how playlists helps musicians to connect with their audience. He said, "Spotify playlists and Spotify charts and Spotify play have become number one tool labels, artists and managers are using in order to break artists and measure success". You can then use those newly gained fans that you received from the playlists to run a Presave Campaign on your next song. The Presave campaign helps you to promote your upcoming music on this platform. This campaign tends to offer incentives to your listeners to encourage them to save your music before the release date.

Independent Curator that helps to drive streams through Playlisting

Getting started with Spotify playlisting may be confusing for upcoming musicians. Therefore you need to work with promoters to get your playlist to several audiences. To get started with Spotify playlisting, you should contact us on http://www.theorendaagency.com/ for proper guide and assistance.

Spotify for Artist

Spotify allows artists to discover who is listening to their music and probably notifies musicians about the latest tools to make available on the platform. When you navigate to your Spotify account as a musician, you should claim your account to gain complete access to every activity going on within your account. You can proceed to claim your account by navigating to the claim icon on your profile page. Spotify will verify your status before giving you complete access to your account.

Spotify for Artist app is designed specifically to help musicians manage, and monitor their songs on the platform. Apple users can visit their apple store and download the app, or they can simply use this link https://apps.apple.com/us/app/spotify-for-artists/id1222021797?ls=1 to get the app. On the other hand, android users can use the google play store and download the app, or they can get the app using this link https://play.google.com/store/apps/details?id=com.spotify.s4a

Why you should verify your Spotify account

There is a need to verify your Spotify account, as this action will convince your audience that you are genuine and real. However, other people may tend to create their accounts with similar names, and your audience may become confused while searching for your profile. When Spotify grants you access to their Spotify for artists app, your profile will be verified automatically and you will get a blue checkmark attached to your profile.

Apple Music for Artist:

Just like Spotify for artists, Apple Music allows musicians to lay claim on their page. They can gain complete access to the page by verifying their pages. Apple music will confirm their identity before granting such a request. To gain access to your Artist account faster, you ought to verify your other social media handle on this platform. However, if you are signed under a Label, your label representative that has the administrative access to your account will prove their relationship with you.

Apple Music

Apple Music is a video streaming service provider created by Apple Inc. This platform is available in over 160 countries and millions of people use this platform to stream over 60 million songs per day.

How Apple Music works for musicians

Musicians use this platform to stream their music to millions of their viewers. Apple Music allows its subscribers to create a profile or follow their favorite musicians to stream their favorite songs online. This implies that Apple users are allowed to pay a monthly subscription to access music on the platform. To add your music on apple music as a single musician, you can contact a distributor to do that for you. However, if you're signed to a label, you will not have a problem with this.

How to use the Apple Music for Artist

Since apple music works only on devices manufactured by Apple Inc, you will be required to get an Apple phone or Mac OS to get started. To lay claim on your Artist page, follow these steps;

1. Get the Apple app installed on your iPhone through this link https://appleid.apple.com/#!&page=signin or sign in using your Mac OS through this link https://artists.apple.com/.

2. If you are yet to join the platform, you should sign up, otherwise, you can sign in to your account and proceed.

3. Navigate to Request Artist Access icon and proceed.

4. Navigate to your iTunes store and copy your artist page, then paste to search.

5. Choose one of your albums to verify your claims.

6. Select your role.

7. Fill the requested application field and wait for feedback.

Amazon Music

Apart from Spotify and Apple Music, Amazon Music is the third-largest online streaming provider. This platform was referred to previously as Amazon MP3. Just like other music distributors, Amazon music is an online streaming platform to connect musicians with their audience. Amazon Music has over 55 million listeners as of January 2020. This number of users has shown that this platform can create better opportunities for musicians.

How to Upload your music to Amazon Library

When it comes to uploading your music to Amazon music, you will have to consider the possibilities of making money from your song. You can work with music distributors if you are a single musician, or your label will do that for you.

You can contact music distributors such as Distrokid, CDBaby, TuneCore, united masters, and many others to get your song on Amazon.

Tidal Music

Tidal music is categorized as subscription-based music. It comes as a music video streaming service provider combined with high definition lossless audio sound. This implies that music video content uploaded on this platform must have special features that will engage the audience. Tidal music came into the limelight in 2014 and its launching was done by Norwegian Public company. However, the company was later purchased by Jay Z.

How to upload your music on Tidal Music Platform

Just like other major platforms, Tidal music will also expect you to work through a music distributor to get your music playing on its platform. Therefore, if you are yet to join a music label, you shouldn't panic as music distributors like Distrokid, CDBaby, TuneCore, united masters, and many others, can help you to execute this task.

Alternative Options

Apart from the above companies, you can check out other music distribution companies such as google play music, Vevo, Napster, Youtube Music, Deezer, Audiomack, and many others.

Best Music Distribution Companies

As a single artist, you should know much about the best music distribution companies that can get your music across several platforms. Below is the list of best music distribution companies you should work with.

1. **Distrokid**: Distrokid was launched in 2013 by an American entrepreneur known as Philip J Kaplan. The company works as an independent digital music distribution service provider. The goal of this distribution company was to help musicians upload their music on all the major music distribution platforms such as Spotify, Apple Music, Amazon Music, Tidal, and many

others. You can proceed to work with them when you visit their website https://distrokid.com/ and contact them.

2. **Cd Baby**: This Independent distribution company has helped over 600,000 artists to upload millions of music on several platforms. The company partners with Spotify and Apple music to serve their clients better. You can reach out to them on https://cdbaby.com/ to get your music uploaded on major music distribution platforms.

3. **Tune Core**: Tune core is a top independent music distribution company that helps artists to sell their music in over 150 major music platforms. They also distribute music to millions of listeners in over 150 countries. Apart from these benefits, Tunecore helps its clients to collect their earnings from youtube and other major platforms. You can contact them on https://www.tunecore.com/ to proceed.

4. **United Masters**: This company was launched in 2017 by Steve Stoute. The company helps artists to push their music to major platforms through advertisement. The company has helped over 50,000 musicians connect with the outside world. You can check out their services on https://unitedmasters.com/.

5. **Ditto Music:** Ditto music is an online music distribution company that helps musicians to

distribute their music to over 160 major music Distribution Companies. You can visit them on https://www.dittomusic.com/.

Alternative Options

Other independent music distribution companies are not mentioned above. They include;

- **Landr**: Visit https://www.landr.com/en/digital-distribution to read more.

- **Record Union**: Navigate to https://www.recordunion.com/ for more details.

- **MondoTune**: Browse https://www.octiive.com/ to get more information.

- **Reverb Nation**: Visit https://www.reverbnation.com/ to connect with them.

- **iMusician:** You can always reach out to them on https://imusiciandigital.com/en/

What Major Music Distribution Platforms pays per stream

When it comes to payment, each major platform has its terms and conditions provided for its users. The payment differs from each other. Some platforms tend to pay higher than others. Below is how these companies pay their users per stream;

S/NO	Platform	Payment Per Stream
	Spotify	$0.00437
	Apple Music	$0.00783
	Amazon Music	$0.00402
	Tidal Music	$0.01284
	Google Play Music	$0.00676
	Napster	$0.019
	Youtube Music	$0.00069
	Pandora	$0.00133
	Deezer	$0.0064

Attend Most Music Conferences

As an upcoming musician, you should make out time to attend every music conference held within your localities and beyond. Most popular musicians tend to grace these conferences to participate or get interviewed. You should consider attending some of these conferences;

1. **SXSW**: South by South by Southwest festival is an annual festival that brings entertainers together. This festival started in 1987, and ever since then, it has expanded and brings top musicians together. The organizers of this conference usually host it in Austin Texas, United States.

2. **Revolt Music Conference (RMC)**: Founded by music executive Sean "P Diddy" Combs this conference is usually graced by popular musicians,entertainers, and label executives. The last revolt submits hosted in Los Angeles was a big success. You should consider attending 2020 submit, as the conference date will be announced at their official website, https://www.revoltsummit.com/.

3. **A3C Festivals**: This festival is an annual festival usually organized in Atlanta US. The purpose of this festival is to unite artists and promote the people's culture. As an upcoming musician, you should join this festival and do your network wisely. You might get a link up for future performance or collaboration.

How to Build Assets as an Upcoming Artist

The goal of every industry is to secure more funds and gain more attention from their targeted audiences. This same goal applies to the music industry as every musician is working extra hard to build assets as they push their music contents across the world. As an upcoming artist, your goal should focus on how to grow your fan base, because the volume of your audience will determine your stand in the industry. Therefore, every musician that wishes to build a great asset in the music industry must deploy the following strategies;

1. **Build an impressive fan base:** Fanbase is the backbone of every successful musician. Your content must match with what your audience wants. In the US, music lovers spent over $40 Billion per year, just to streamline their favorite music. From this example, you can discover that music lovers now spend a lot of money just to listen to their favorite musicians. You can capitalize on your effort in growing your fan base, as your success in the music industry highly depends on them.

2. **Partner with Brands**: Top companies and organizations are seriously searching for the best opportunity to push their brand to a fresh audience. When you have an impressive audience, many companies will love to push their brand product to your audience. You can

make a lot of money to build a better asset with this strategy. You can feature brand products on your music videos, or post as a regular vlog video on your social media platforms.

3. **Present the Brands is a different way**: Before you partner with a brand, you ought to have background knowledge on how other musicians promote brands in their music videos. Bigger brands are always out there watching your videos, and when you represent the brands differently, you can get bigger projects from those top companies.

4. **Product Placement in Music Videos**: Top companies are willing to pay artists who promote their products in their music videos. You should look out for brand sponsorship whenever you make a move to shoot your videos. For instance, Beat by Dre pays musicians just to add their products to their music videos.

Some notable examples of how Musicians partnered with apparel Brands

1. **Kanye West with Adidas**: Kanye West is famous in the music industry, and He has partnered with several top brands which in turn helped him to build a huge asset outside the music industry. Adidas confirmed in 2013 a collaboration deal with Kanye West on new shoe designs. However,

in February 2015, the new shoe design was revealed by the company. The Adidas Yeezy was distributed across the world. As time goes on, the company manufactured more designs and made great sales from the product. West was not left behind, as he was paid for his collaboration deal.

2. **Travis Scott Partnership with Nike**: Nike is popularly known for their footwear designs. In October 2017, Travis Scott announced his partnership with Nike on his Instagram post. He has featured Nike in their VaporMax Sneaker and Airforce 1 Model Campaigns.

Some notable examples of how Musicians built their own apparel brand.

1. **Kanye West with Yeezy Brand**: Even though Ye partnered with Adidas for Yeezy, he still owns 100% of the brand. This is a massive advantage for him, especially since the company is worth 3 Billion dollars. At any moment in time he can sell the company and cash out. The Yeezy brand has gained fame all over the globe, with everyone dying to get their hands on a pair. Building your own unique brand can take a lot of time and effort , but in the end it'll be well worth it.

2. **Justin Bieber with Drew House:** Justin Bieber

started to gain insane amounts of attention at a young age. With the help of Scooter Braun, Bieber was able to take his career to places he couldn't even imagine. With all his new found fame, Justin saw an opportunity to expand and establish his brand, which is why he started his own clothing line called Drew House. Partnerships can be extremely beneficial, but it comes nowhere close to having full ownership and control over your brand. He took advantage of the fan base he already had and found ways to create yet another stream of income for himself, while simultaneously promoting his music.

Chartmetric

Chartmetric is a modern method of tracking, analyzing, and measuring music data in all social media platforms. It helps to simplify the digital music outlook as it connects music data from several platforms for its users. Musicians can now channel their focus to the latest trends and take advantage of it. Chartmetric helps artists to unlock their potential analytics on how to connect better with their fans across all platforms. It tends to provide reliable music data, fan base support, and an innovative approach towards making smarter music decisions. With Chartmetric, artists can easily discover all the playlist that contains their music.

Why Fiverr is Necessary for Artists

Fiverr is an online freelancing market place. You can buy literally any service from this platform. As an independent artist, you will require a lot of services such as Cover art, Instagram Layout, Graphics designs, and a lot more to back up your music career. You can connect with experts on this platform to get the best service. To get started, visit https://www.fiverr.com/ to explore the platform. However, you will have to register on this platform before you can navigate to its pages and connect with your service providers. The general services required by musicians include;

- **Photo Editing**: Every musician must have professional photo editors to give a final touch to their regular uploads. To connect with photo editors on Fiverr, visit https://www.fiverr.com/search/gigs?query=photo%20editing&source=main banner&acmpl=1&search in=everywhere&search-autocomplete-original-term=photo%20&search-autocomplete-available=true&search-autocomplete-type=suggest&search-autocomplete-position=0

- **Cover Art**: Cover art helps to attract your audience to listen to your music content. Therefore, you will need to define your music album with impressive cover art. To connect with the right service providers on Fiverr, Visit https://www.fiverr.com/search/gigs?query=cover%20art%20for%20musicians&source=top-bar&search_in=everywhere&search-autocomplete-original-term=cover%20art%20for%20musicians

- **Instagram Layouts**: Instagram layouts are an essential need for every musician on Instagram. Visit https://www.fiverr.com/search/gigs?query=instagram%20layout&source=top-bar&acmpl=1&search_in=everywhere&search-autocomplete-original-term=instagram%20la&search-autocomplete-available=true&search-autocomplete-type=suggest&search-autocomplete-position=0

- **Graphic designs**: From time to time, you will need several designs to meet up with a particular need. To connect with professional designers on Fiverr, visit https://www.fiverr.com/search/gigs?query=graphic%20designs&source=top-bar&search_in=everywhere&search-autocomplete-original-term=graphic%20designs

REFERENCES

https://thenextweb.com/insider/2015/11/20/9-things-to-help-your-youtube-video-go-viral/

https://theinfluencermarketingfactory.com/5-ways-to-get-your-music-to-go-viral-on-tiktok/

https://rafflepress.com/how-to-go-viral-on-instagram/

https://www.musicindustryhowto.com/how-to-use-tik-tok-for-musicians/

https://trillervids.tumblr.com/Howtousetriller

https://blog.hootsuite.com/social-media-advertising/

https://later.com/blog/tiktok-challenges/

https://influencermarketinghub.com/top-tiktok-hashtags/

https://medium.com/@contact.junelewis/list-of-10-independent-spotify-playlist-curators-you-can-submit-your-music-to-dbbbe178ec32

https://blog.landr.com/everything-musicians-need-know-digital-music-distribution/

https://www.dittomusic.com/blog/how-much-do-music-streaming-services-pay-musicians

https://gleam.io/blog/spotify-pre-save/

http://everythingexperiential.businessworld.in/article/Top-10-music-festivals-of-the-world/07-06-2018-151412/

https://www.chartmetric.com/

https://artists.spotify.com/guide/spotify-for-artists

https://artists.apple.com/support/42-claim-your-account

https://blog.symphonicdistribution.com/2019/11/reasons-every-musician-should-be-using-twitch/

https://diymusician.cdbaby.com/social-media/twitch-for-musicians/

https://promo.ly/spotify-for-artists-playlists/

www.ingramcontent.com/pod-product-compliance
Lightning Source LLC
Chambersburg PA
CBHW060945040426
42445CB00011B/1010